Songs for a Son

Songs for a Son

Robert L. Peters

W · W · NORTON & COMPANY · INC ·

NEW YORK

First Edition

Library of Congress Catalog Card No. 66-23985

Published simultaneously in Canada by
George J. McLeod Limited, Toronto

"Kittens" first appeared in *The Fiddlehead*,
"Ceremony" in *Western Humanities Review*,
"Brain and Brother," "Fern, Moth, and Hand," "Dance"
and "Song for a Son" in the *Sausalito-Belvedere Gazette*,
and "A Reply" in *Prairie Schooner*.

Printed in the United States of America

1 2 3 4 5 6 7 8 9 0

FOR

Jean

and Rob, Meredith, Amity, and Jeff

Contents

Part Three

Wings without feathers creaking in the sun,
The close dirt dancing on a sunless stone
God's night and day: down this space He has smiled,
O who would take the vision from the child?

—Theodore Roethke

Songs for a Son

Prelude

Life
presses on the brain
shoots in its mercury
sets the patient
quivering.

Brain
absorbs, declares, informs
and, drawn-lipped autocrat,
locks in all speech,
all scenes, all taste
and smell, dumps
everything.

Part One

1 / Motif

I

In winter
a bird drops
from a bough;
the snow entombs him
wraps him in.

When spring
unlocks the forest
feathers stiffen
wings collapse
pinoil grease
thaws and dries
beak whitens
eyejuice melts
internally
flesh softens
a purple stain.

II

These are fragments
of pain, stalactites
of the heart doomed
to melt, leveling panic
the jab in the guts
the slick vein leaping
over my hand
perplexed sick
over its branchings
multiform.

2 / Theme

I

Dampwinter
smoke and snow

exposed tree roots

the bridge

fins flickering
beneath the ice
of the greenish river:

gone gone utterly
    all gone

with white mice and bones
found on a beach

snowbeaten fur and
soft green patch
of skeleton and flesh

birds' wings
frozen on the grass

columns
cracked and chipped
like porcelain,
overwhelmed.

II

I call your name, son,
festooned and touched
with amber in my mind:
Richard. Peace.

The apple turns to ash,
the slumbering worm
begins to swell, stir,
prepares his rubbery mouth
for the assault.

I run a cinder
through my palm,
firing the ember

and my flesh
burns as
heart drains
its fear—
flick of a
worm's beak.

The sun comes down.
It stamps its lamp
against my brain.
I shielded, shield my eyes
against the glare! Where
are you gone, son?
Where? Where?

3 / Report

I turned you, Richard,
kissed your neck
to wake you
from that fever-breaking sleep
and saw
your blue cracked lip
the stark death-mark.

4 / Hospital

Wheeze away, O green steel tank!
Breathe, gray nosecup set
over the hardening cartilage
of his nose!

        (Unsheeted form
        on a wheeled-in table:
        robe, fresh urinestain
        on the pajamas—designs
        of tugboats, bedroom
        slippers.)

Mechanical sustainer! Push those lungs,
inflate them, swell them! Shock them
into breath again!

        (Bent heads
        hands probing
        detecting
        over the
        wheeled-in table.)

O neutral doctor! O delicate finger
laboring! O pluck the heart (fat
and vein) blood-fretted jewel; strum
melody

        (He does not breathe!)

dredge out the heart and
shake it, slap it, bathe it
in the glare of the
stainless light

above the wheeled-in table;
massage it   prick it
be brutal, hand, be god
prick the quiescent
                                        immobile
                                                    gem

5 / Word

The word *death*
is far more desolate
than any stream
set anywhere in nature
or in heaven, more
fragrant than radium
in pitchblend: to eat
a hand, devour an eye;
to scorch the sour
vein dangling the heart
from the chest chamber,
the breath from the throat,
the ear from its stirrup.

6 / Transformation

I know
that between death's
hot coppery sides
the slime of birth
becomes a chalky
track of bone
compressed in time
to slate, or gneiss,
or marble—pressed
lifeless into stone.

They will never remember
one so young, or one so
mirthful, or one so
quiet in his bed.

7 / Scene

Winter has a dark theme.
It leaves me watching.
My need
            is unsatisfied.

There is an eye out there.
Water slips from its rim.
The eyeball has a
clogged center—
the heart-stalk of a
lettuce plant developing
seed.

Fog creeps to the eye,
rests flat beneath it,
absorbs the water, juice,
which drips now
like honey running.

Eyeball turns
from me. A simple scene,
overwhelming.

Winter has a dark theme.

8 / Dance

A brain danced in the wind
A natural shape for a natural
mind—its motions diaphanous.
Outrageous performer!
    no rod, stick, string,
    or invisible hand.
Clouds rose behind it.

Music I could not hear
(but only imagined)
whirled into sound:
tunes for an oboe
tambourine and violin.
A brain danced in the wind.

There were no trees at hand.
Birds settled to earth
and slept on warm stones
wing-fast. A brain
danced in the wind.

9 / Brain and Brother

This brain
this fist of sponge
enthroned in the attic
is a center, a space
for blood, venom, and
for love. It waits
on its dais. Feel it
tingle, receiving news,
framing messages: notes
gathered from vines
over the eaves, from
each mouse nibbling
the sheaves, from each
trick or treat, all
candies flung from
the parade.
Marvellous
sponge! unlike your
brother locked at the
bottom of the sea, or
on a green shelf placed
with neptune-weed,
suspended for effect,
a rock in place,
a niche of time, mindless,
without a prayer to
deity or fish or golden
ass or ancestors interred
beneath a fireplace.

10 / Fever

We did not seek
this monument, nor
ever wished it:
bed, drawn shade,
steamer vaporing
the room, peeling
the sill, smoking
the lungs (slender
ferny tracks
born of an ancient sea),
and fever, loathsome
traveler with his
pack all rolled,
his blanket ready
for the tryst, a
true fire, reedy,
igniting, his
destination
our son's dear
capital, his helpless
brain!

11 / Memory

I swallow,
aid memory (the mind's
gelatin) to salve the
eyelid gashed, the
cells ripped like muslin,
and vision bleeding,
the inkwell wholly dry.

I wait, I lift the
corner of the tape
and spy my wound
so pale, as pale as
lungs burnished
with alcohol, the
red petals of a
scar, a wet eye,
winking, winking.

I sing for you Richard
and for your coatbutton
loose, the untied shoes,
the collar open at the throat,
nor would the bathrobe close,
the chord was lost,
the nurse had failed
to see . . .

12 / Wound

The wound is closing in:
flakes, gold horny substance,
salmon ridge, miniscule
orange craters
bearing red centers.

I unlatch
the surgeon's clips,
grind glass between flat stones,
impale a splinter
underneath my nail,
lift the
hardened corners
of the wound, tear
flesh into strips,

endure nausea,
whorls of hurt,
and free the gelatin,
the cells, the salmon ridge,
and drop in
glass, sand,
bits of chaff,
press,
release fresh blood,
watch it spurt.

Part Two

13 / Wall

Let's wait beside
the nonsense wall,
all dread: white flaking
bricks, dust for tears,
for scissors, paste.

"Spratt and wife," I say
to call you back. "Cow,
dog, moon, and spoon," I
try again. The air
flows hollow. "Burst, fat,
hungering George who flew
away, was never seen." I
laugh, assume a troll's voice:
"The Human Pole, a string
of a man with all his
buttons lost, nibbling
a fat brown roll; Tucker
wanting supper, the stolen
tarts, the jack of hearts
snapped flat against the
deck, breaded honey, black-
bird, the nurse's blear
proboscis stuck to an icy
line, Riding Hood's basket
adorned with silk, with milk,
the wolf's meal, the squeal,
and grandma freed—grotesque
and happy birth!"

14 / Opacity

Black night
backs the reflection
in the window.

On stark mornings
with the wild sun
streaming there is
no glass, no opacity.

But at night
with the moths striking,
this book in my hand,
the pen moving,
my face in the glass
darkened

I am the mirror's back.
I lend opacity, and
crawl toward speech.

15 / A Reply

(to William Carlos Williams)

When pushed to say
each man declines
to call himself a dog,
or one of a pack of dogs
("just another dog
among a lot of dogs").

Granted scant imaginations
            unaided
by the reading of verse,
or by the taste of death,
there will remain,
            nevertheless,
two or three
            who see themselves as
            rabbits pursued
            tree grubs spied
            by the flicker
            deer licking wounds.
In any one of these
there is no just another.

And
at a next remove,
fancies that love difference
will seize upon dream
will freeze
            the hare on the trail
            the bee seeking honey
            the doe the waterfield
            of lilies.

16 / Preserve

Again
I can see that mass of trees:
moist veins
racked against the sky
mortal backdrop
for a world of
twig, black leaf, and
large hill riddled
with mange and rot;

and beneath your feet
a bridge, snowy,
with crisp flakes
spun from the hooves
of does in troll-land
frightened for their young.

There, dazzled by
blue light, by ice,
you sped through the
morning: your boot
buckles clicking and
red mittens pointing
(hands on film)
toward each frozen
wonder of the trail:

globes of cowfat
tied in mesh and
stuck with seeds
(corn, oat, sunflower,
rice) swung from branches;

coconut skulls
filled with meal,
fists of oak, wood-knobs
smeared with grease,
and rinds of orange,
and powdered milk
in bottles, to feed
the birds.

A globe
turned in the wind.
Birds shivered
as we passed.
And on you ran.

I called out to you,
called out to you, boy,
saw your prints and joy
skim through the water
spin like the bugs
we saw in summer
on the drugged lake,
flung pebbles at,
begged time to flounder.

On you sped
through woods and brush
passed the pike-weed
marsh, the beaver dam.

I caught your sparkle
toward the rounding bay
drenched with sun
fisherman.

"Keep, keep within sight
of land," I cried;
"of every riddle, joy,
the pains of Christmas,
Easter, grandma's house,
the fair"—the prompting
died.

"The enemy!" you screamed,
and with your sister
leaped the brook
a month before the close,
before
            the trap sprang
before
            the ice rang in
            and froze your
            mouth, heart,
            glorious eyes and limbs:
            ice-flowers of death,
            blue, exfoliate utterly!

17 / Easter

Meredith gave up her doll
last night. You would not
have known his face, so
aged it was. Soap was
hopeless. His rag cheeks
were cancerous. His lips,
still smiling, mocked
decay. Raggedy-Andy,
Raggedy-Andy. Meredith
wrote a note: "Spirit
him off to Easterland."
She kissed him. "One
more day to live," she
said. "One night to live."
She left him in his chair.
By morning
he was gone.

Play with him, Richard.
She asks it.
Keep his gray face.
Kiss all death
from his buttoned eyes.
Kiss sleep from his mouth.

18 / Bones in a Valley

More than a life
is sliced by death.

Death severs crumbs
hacks the brain's leaf
through, numbs
what was solid
devours one meal
grabs for another.

Glutton! your butchering knife
is keen. But you lie, death.
It is not true what you
prompt me to say: "To lose
my son's image
reveals my own
wish to die."

These are cinders at my feet
bones in a valley
jostling

flames brighten around me
my toe raises smoke.

What have I lost?
What is ravished that was mine?
What burned away?

19 / Song for a Lost Son

My son's image
was painted on sand.

The wind from off the lake
bears me no news of him,
nor of his impression.

Was it arrogance to think
that I could hold his features?

I had set them in memory,
fashioned cameos for the
mind, had seen that face at will,
in various attitudes, transforming
me—when he was alive.

But I am blind!
Unable to create a brow,
a lash, the hollow down
the back of the neck,
the throat!

Look.
Those trees hold nothing
in their branches. Those rushes
by the lake, so rife with
blackbirds, hold nothing:
            Mist faces,
            faces in shrouds,
            faces in clouds . . .
Water has worn the cameos down

20 / Summer

I leaped from the boat
and (crux of a summer's
courage) forged on
through deep water,
thorax clenched like steel
arm plunging
passed scarlet eyes
rocks, slime
and fat lungs
loaded with water—

they were orange
and ferny,
perfect,
wavering in
an ocean, the branches
mine and all
of my children's.

21 / Morning

I

In the soft hours
in the first sift of
gray light the
first cars rumbling
I stand glance
toward the yard
past the trellis
where you played
turned stones for worms
replaced the stones;
to the swings, the seats
you painted, splattering
the cracked planks
and the chinning bar
with gold; to the
gay slab boats
and the machines
built from magazines
torn, pasted, placed
on stilts of tinkertoys
and brown blocks
propped by rocks;
to the mix you stirred
that fatal morning
seated on the earth
by the shed
under the leafless oak:
Porridge, you exclaimed;
magic food
meant to sprout

trees of ice cream,
flowers of balloons,
crayons, mice, gilt
shrubs and wishbones,
kittens, dogs.

II

Dawn strikes the oak.
Gloss sheens the lake,
spring's tulip-hue.

(And there is the sand.
The tunnels for the mice
are still intact. The
twigs for trees
you stuck in mousetown
wait for spring.)

A pool glistens
near the ageratum:
winter's drizzle,
chill sterility.

22 / Encounter

You heard, son,
the ominous
beat-skip-beat
of the heart

and scrambled down
from the yellow swing
bearing mouse in hand

and saw the red trickle,
the straightened tail,
the eye glazed pink,
the paws curled in.

23 / Oh, Cabin Mice!

Frenzied by the smell
of stale bread, jam,
and meat locked up
for the season, cabin mice
in the dead of winter
scamper over carpets,
up and down cupboards,
beat paths around the
fireplace, discover
envelopes of grain
poisoned pellets
prepared for them.

They ignore
tails and whiskers,
female heat, lice
in their fur, the
puddle of snow-water
under the door,
decree sharp teeth,
squeal, squirm, nip,
and draw mouseblood,
leap over each other,
sate themselves,
grow tranquil at last,
serene, tummied (the
tits of the mother mice
bursting with fresh-
pastured milk from
the granary), make
lingering copulations

just before
the advent of
slow blood
deterioration
of cell walls
hemophilia
falsely induced
swelling up
of hot breath
charred lungs, blood
seeping

and the trip
outside, into the cold,
away from the
suffocating
cabin eaves.

And a bright aster
forms at the mouth,
snowbloom, leaves
blooming in the snow,
and a bright calendula
unfolds
        beneath the tail.

Part Three

24 / Snow

I shall never touch snow
and not see your plaid coat
and the blue cap
with flaps like
small rabbits
by your ears.

25 / Turtles and Mice

As we grope, son,
seek you again,
your coat, laces,
rusting skates, and
black stuffed seal
who truly died beside you,
hugged beneath
your stiffening arm,
and seek you
in your squiggles
made on paper,
the turtles you cut out,
bent the legs of
so they'd walk,
and placed them
on a farm with mice,
blind, a troll waits,
his spiked head
turned toward
the west
his eye a sapphire
in the dusk.

26 / Troll

Who is trampling
on my bridge?

Richard is my name.

Where's your father?
Where is he?

Coming later, not
today.

I can't wait! I know
that tale!

I'm coming, Richard,
Richard Nathaniel Frank!
Ready or not, there's no
time out this game!

27 / Responsibility

Never tell that tale,
bright child. Never say
the fantasies, for they do
come true. They transpire
on mild mornings when the
pale spindly woods mourn
for the sap locked
in their roots.

I am your troll,
bright child tramping
on the bridge: for who
has seen the wind?
and who
among the leaves
hangs trembling?

28 / Resolution

We hang:
plump leaves
swung from a
summer-seared branch
suspended.

Tentworms, a whole
prismatic range,
spin gauze
will soon cover us
smother us:
slick, slick, hear them
chew.

Death sweeps through.
Burrs cling
to the billowy gauze
of that
proud gown.

29 / Kittens

The kittens came tonight,
the ones you'd wished for
when you broke
the hen's breast-bone
that Wednesday, death-day
morning. You had asked for
plump dark woolly cats
with eyes like olives,
glossy; cats tumbling
on the floor soundless,
pricking at string,
lapping up blue milk,
their abdomens
as tight as udders.

This was the scene:
the brindled cat squirmed
beneath the chair,
whined, rose, and
plunged, spread-legged
through the room
to find a box, a hat,
a place by a commode

for birth. We set
a blue crate for her,
spread down a towel
and waited. Two
shaky forms appeared
smeared with blood,
fur wet like licorice,
eyelids swollen.
The mother screamed
(an angry rip of cloth),
glanced swiftly back,
impelled by burning muscle
found the wet cowering lumps,
peeled then swallowed
their rubbery translucent
coats, lent her tongue
to smear the wobbling
panting forms all shiny
bound with feebleness;
ink-black they fell
into a land of honey:
then dropped the third
and last.

But earlier, on wish-day
death-day, poised
on my mound of sand,
I'd said "No cats,"
and quelled your joy
with news of chance
loose from the zoo
against you: "No
mice, no toads, no turtles,
salamanders, frogs"—
I made a catalogue—

"they die.
Their little toes
curl up like leaves,
their waxy eyes go shut,
their tails hang limp
their whiskers droop."

Dreading each death's
advent, I sought to
spare you. Each lost
pet might break deep,
deep within your heart,
might crystallize its
red wet velvet sides
into long beads of rice
to feed the worm—
or snap them into
tears like seeds
to break on stone:
each death a buzz, an
eel's tail slapped
against your knee,
a blue, a fatal jolt!

In proof I said,
"Count up your pets:
the molting snake
gashed half-way to
its tail, remember
him?" We speared Snake
food (some, living,
bled on toothpicks)
and thrust them past
the forked and flicking
palate, the svelte

unhinging jaws.
But Snake died
rolled like an earthworm
in his leaves! And you,
Meredith, and Rob
spun panegyrics,
wrought wreaths of
golden asps with wings
like flames for borders.

Then Mouse: remember
how you bore him
through the yard
wrapped in his hard
leaf-shroud, his green tail
sprinkling mortality
like ivy-juice
all over you that day?
You brought a metal pail,
spilled water in the hole
torn by your rusted shovel.
You wept and gracefully
placed Mouse beneath a
tulip root. Two nails
formed a cross, a fallen
leaf the saviour. There
Mouse still lies set
by your own hands
firmly into place—
unless the earth with
acid formed from oaks
has decomposed his bones,
like yours, to ash,
and slipped all down
between packed grains

of quartzite, sandstone,
beryl, smoothed out with
lime and all the other
flavors of an earthy crypt.

But all my scare
of zoo and deep-felled
nightmare failed
and would not settle
in your brain's mailed
small hole for fear,
where clung invisible
the hung smoke of the
sleeping fatal fever.
I smiled broadly from
the table, hitched up
my belt, enjoyed your
able innocence, bade you
break the bone and gladly
eat your wish.

With shy delight you
seized the dish, took up
and sprung the wing, turned
it like stone to see through
in the light, sprung it wide,
asked it to snap, to softly
free your wish:
        jarring the light-hung
        particles of dust
        caught near the window
        the bone did break!

Our house now
crawls with kittens.

They tumble, stumble, run,
find bits of sun,
find mother's udders,
mews. They lick themselves
waver on unfirm claws,
do all the acts,
make all the gestures that
you knew live kittens make.

I'm glad you took
these facts with you
into the night! I'd
rather have you take
these kitten facts along
than all the history
you never came to know,
the shouts of passion,
war; the violence of cars;
the poetry that never
broke itself against
your ears. O
that there had been more!

30 / Cat, Word, and Fern

More.
The word rolls over
its feet in air
and claws
the turbulence of heart,
O heart! The claws
stiffen, curl in
like fronds
against the stem.
The claws drop free.
The word dies.
The fern molds.

31 / Fern, Moth, and Hand

The fern molds into bits,
syllables spilled out
upon the yeasty earth,
spoors. The tattered leaves
boast tips of red. Nearby,
an orange fallow bulb
lures a crisp moth
hungering for his com-
plement (the moth finds
death) in the pale buttery
stem. His wings flutter.
He flings himself, bruised
eye, antenna crippled—
a stick half-broken under
water, the bubbles breaking
past. The soft tail curls,
burning, curls toward the
startled vanquished eye.
Red chaff crumbles from
the spoor; the cheese
from the spoor-head follows.
The flesh stem splinters,
the eye goes out, the wing's
eye dissolves, the antennae
shake, straighten, their
glory clapped shut.

Son, what is the stone
cast over us? whose wrist
flexed the shafted muscle
clad in mail?

Whose finger aimed
the flinted point?
What have we lost, son?
Can you say, son?
Son, can you say?

32 / Boat

I

The waves shiver.
I glance down
and see the shell
of a rotted boat.
Is that a shadow
or a boat? Does a fish
spin, stroke past,
brush the crumbling
sides? There is
metal down there—
or is it a bone casting up
glare? It is noon;
there is nightmare.

II

A petal from a saffron bell
drops from a bush. My image
on the lake rushes,
rushes after the oar.
My hook trails, forgotten,
free of log and weed. Fearing
the depths I pull toward
shore. The wind moves.
Broad skies move. The dour
partridge floats above the
wet nose of the fox. A
dragonfly quivers
over an inch of web
jewelled with the debris
of wings.

III

The boat is beached.
(The boat is bleached.)
Oars rest on the seat.
The fish splatters behind me
where the water gathers.

"Fish." I grasp its sides.
"What's your desire?"

There is blood. I have
ripped a finger. A red pearl
drops into the water.
Another strikes the wing
of a moth caught in a web
beside the trail. The wing
shakes, shakes. Sweet blood
drops from my hand.
I walk on fallen needles.
There is a lake inside me.

33 / The Sun Declares the Morning

The sun declares the morning.
Wind turns the leaves
as jays blare
and a truck whirrs
climbing the mountain
carrying supplies.
(The stream to the lake
is dry again.)

Squirrels race
through manzanita brush.
A hummingbird
probes for juices,
and flower bells, fat,
drop off. The air
grows still. An orange
cat treads the woods
oblivious of jays and
squirrels; his tail
switches, volatile.

There were more lights on
in the cabins last night
(the weekend approaches).
They will open a valve
soon, run water from the
pumphouse, keep the lake
at a respectable level.

34 / Flight

Slight vapors and thin fogs
speed on at these high altitudes.

Clouds shroud the sky,
the jet's wing, and Ship's

Rock below. The desert bears
a wintry look; chill banks of

cloud boil with snow, fill
rifts of light with gauze.

Time pales, slips with the
ease of an oiled piston.

Shadows below, cloud shadows
lavender, clamor for space,

float—loud designs on the
orchid land. There is no

ether here for souls. We
skim through mortally.

The plane shakes. Far below
are patches of red rock,

a painted desert truly
for foundering upon. Fog

settles in. The driving
engines waft us through,
bouncing, sparkling. Speed
seems to rest. It is all

incredible. You
are not here!

35 / Ceremony

I

I take you from the church,
in a brown leathery
cube. I cannot read
the label, the facts
of ash. A car, passing,
throws sun against
my face—a clarion.

I ask for a shovel.
"No trouble," says the
preacher. I follow,
pass through
Gethsemane.

We have trouble
with the shovel:
gone from its place—
a plain fact askew.

I fear that the winds
will howl soundless
again.

We find a spade,
though not the one
we wished; and I
lead the way
to a bush on a
rolling slope
set with rock

like the fringe
of a well.
The crown of the
green bush wavers.

I open the box:
a sack, translucent,
crammed with scraps
of brown black white
and yellow bone.
I test the weight,
press the sack to my
cheek, hold it
to my eyes.

Sun streams through,
turns that ivory to
gold, that pale pale
white to blue, those bits
of brown to red!

II

I break the earth
(the spade moves well).
I prune a root
and smooth the hole.
I press the earth
by hand, drop in
a leaf, harbinger,
and kneel.
I crumble-in loam.
As grains slip through
I hunger to count them,
I hunger to count them.

I hope for silence,
vision, a shimmering
saint bearing a twig
studded with emeralds,
a gift.

Richard, Richard,
there was snow that day
and sun enough
to dazzle empires
when you ran laughing
beside the frosty lake,
mortal, lovely, mine.

36 / The Beach

And now,
wherever I walk
heel and soleprint
(saltdrenched)
stir the
rotted eyestalks
of lobsters, crunch
marooned shells . . .
Look! There is a
creature on the beach,
brine gone forever.
There are purple arms,
six at least. Furious,
it sets each limb
and hoists its body,
blue bulb, above
its arms flared out,
defies lethal air,
element, and for a
moment, swells
then bursts, shoots
forth ink, curls in its
tentacles, rests,
becomes a glob
which the sun will
bleach, erase: it
grows extinct,
is not.

37 / Calm

Long weeks have passed.
We have changed homes.
Rob seldom says your name,
though in his way, his
inability to crush a moth,
torment a frog, there is
a quickening. Meredith's
wound lies covered. The
designs she drew,
the morbid valentines,
bright witches burning
children, cats devouring
sandwiches of mice,
are gone at last from
her repertoire. Jeff is
too young to know;
he walks with us
with the aura
that was yours. Amity,
two years older,
adopted, knows the fact
of your departure, turns
it in her hand, growing
colder, like some jewel,
some bit of colored sand.

38 / Coda

I

Stars burst,
pin back the sable
for a glance, then fade.

Petals drop from the vine
and the pink grape blackens,
the fig contains the worm,
leaves yellow and drop;

rust swallows the metal
frames supporting.

Beside the lake the beaver
slap their tails. In the
deep lake fish glimmer.

On the water wild geese
wait. Tomorrow their
keen breasts shall beat
streams of stars.

You loved it here!

II

Our thrusts
are scarcely marble;
they crumble. (There is
no private art; we write
what we can.) Our leapings

fade; so does our burbling
mirth. Our begging and
begetting, they too pass
over the fury of the hour.

What we seek, what binds us,
is a wish to share with
sleek beasts waiting
in the fields, all turned
head to head, toward the
waning sun, a semblance
of calm.

RICHARD NATHANIEL FRANK PETERS

Delaware, Ohio, Sept. 18, 1955—
Ferndale, Michigan, Feb. 10, 1960

Robert L. Peters was born in Eagle River, Wisconsin, and received his B.A., M.A., and Ph.D. degrees from the University of Wisconsin. He is at the present time Professor of Victorian Literature at the University of California in Riverside, California. His other books include *Victorians on Literature and Art; The Crowns of Apollo: Swinburne's Principles of Literature and Art;* and *The Letters of John Addington Symonds* (with Professor Herbert Schueller of Wayne State University). Professor Peters is married and has four children.

Peters
Songs for a son

Date Due
